Strategic Levers to Enable E-business Transformations

Strategic Levers to Enable E-Business
Transformations

Jeanne W. Ross, Cynthia Beath,
V. Sambamurthy, Mark Jepson

May 2000

CISR WP No, 310
Sloan WP No 4119

©2000 Massachusetts Institute of Technology All rights reserved

Center for Information Systems Research
Sloan School of Management
Massachusetts Institute of Technology
77 Massachusetts Avenue, E40-193
Cambridge, MA 02139-4307

MASSACHUSETTS INSTITUTE
OF TECHNOLOGY

JUL 1 3 2001

LIBRARIES

CISR Working Paper No. 310

Title: Strategic Levers to Enable E-Business Transformations

Author: Jeanne W. Ross, Cynthia Beath, V. Sambamurthy, Mark Jepson

Date: May 2000

Abstract: Established businesses are trying to take advantage of the opportunities and minimize the threats presented by e-business. Although e-business has emerged as a strategic imperative for many firms, we found that vision and strategy paled in importance compared to learning and implementation in the process of transforming to an e-business organization. Regardless of their strategic objectives in pursuing e-business (e.g., increased efficiency, enhanced customer or supplier relationships), firms are finding that the transformation from bricks-and-mortar to clicks-and-mortar requires them to learn new ways of organizing and managing their operations, and new ways of applying and investing in information technology. In this report we describe findings from 30 firms in different stages of e-business maturity. These findings suggest that firms can pull three strategic levers to enhance their learning and facilitate their transformation

- IT Infrastructures
- E-Business Governance Structures
- IT Product and Service Delivery

We describe how these levers can be operated and then discuss the obstacles and enablers associated with those levers. Finally, we discuss follow-on research questions emerging from this research

18 Pages

This paper is also available as Sloan Working Paper No 4119

Strategic Levers to Enable
E-Business Transformations

Introduction

The new economy has disrupted old assumptions about how individuals and firms conduct business transactions As capital markets and the business press lavish attention on the dot-coms and their new business models, established firms are responding with e-business initiatives of their own Unlike their dot-com counterparts, however, they have both the benefit and the burden of legacy business processes and physical assets

While e-business is ultimately a business concern, part of what makes e-business challenging is its heavy dependence on information technology The effect at most firms has been a significant increase in the strategic importance of IT This is especially problematic in firms where senior executives have never possessed an appreciation of the strategic relevance of IT Transforming from a bricks-and-mortar business model to a clicks-and-mortar model is an exercise that most established organizations are beginning and so now is a good time to ask what early lessons have been learned and how can they be applied in the future? This report examines the key IT-related issues associated with developing an e-business competency

The Research Study

This study examined the processes by which firms are incorporating e-business into their business models. We solicited participation from firms of a range of sizes in a variety of industries and at different stages of e-business implementation In total we talked with e-business and IT executives at 30 U S and European companies about their e-business initiatives, the IT investments that supported those initiatives, and the apparent outcomes of their efforts

Data was collected between October 1999 and March 2000 in hour-long telephone interviews At 18 of the firms we interviewed both a business executive and an IT manager with key responsibility for e-business. At 12 firms, we talked with either the head of e-commerce or the IT executive responsible for e-commerce In total we conducted 48 interviews at the 30 firms The firms ranged in size from under $500,000 (US) to over $10 billion (US) in sales. All were conducting business transactions on the web, but for most of the firms web transactions represented less than 10% of their revenues. Among our firms, a few had established web-based e-business capabilities as early as 1995, while others had begun as recently as October 1999 On average their e-business experience was about 28 months A list of the firms that participated in the study is included in the Appendix

The *Bricks-and-Mortar* to *Clicks-and-Mortar* Transformation

The firms in the study emphasized that they wanted to integrate e-business initiatives into their existing organizations Whatever their transformation strategy nearly everyone we talked to noted that the hard part was learning how to transform themselves

---

This research report was prepared by Jeanne Ross, MIT Center for Information Systems Research, Cynthia Beath, University of Texas, V Sambamurthy, University of Maryland, and Mark Jepson, IBM Global Services The authors would like to thank IBM and MIT's Center for Information Systems Research for their joint sponsorship

Two had spun off Internet businesses, but most wanted to leverage, where appropriate, the competencies that had made them successful in the past. In all the firms in the sample, the transition to e-business is best characterized as incremental rather than radical, although most of the respondents indicated that the integration of e-business initiatives would change—and in some cases already had changed—their organizations in fundamental ways

Many of the firms were driven to their e-business initiatives by competitive threats One CIO explained, "We feel we are vulnerable to any 14-year-old working out of his garage." Another IT executive noted that his firm's entré into e-business was a reluctant response to the persistent admonitions of financial analysts But some had viewed the web as a strategic opportunity from the outset, and even those that had entered reluctantly were starting to view the internet less as a competitive threat and more as a strategic weapon.

> This vision is a strategic shift from thinking in terms of a process that is a set of transactions to a process that is relationship based. It cuts to the heart and soul of the marketing process and it's about redefining customer service totally We want "quality revenue" which is the revenue that is the most valuable to us in the long run. It's customers that are easy to serve, not those that are problematic or costly to serve We want to move our high priced inventory, not distressed inventory
>
> —Head of Distribution

E-Business Outcomes

Respondents typically sought four different types of e-business outcomes (Figure 1)

1 Increased efficiency—cutting costs through streamlined processes;
2 Enhanced/redefined customer relationships—classifying customers for specific services and ensuring a positive customer experience;
3 Enhanced/redefined supplier relationships—creating new alliances, refocusing or eliminating non-value-added relationships, and
4 New products and services—identifying and selling new capabilities, most often web-based This involved entering new markets

Figure 1

The E-Business Learning Cycle

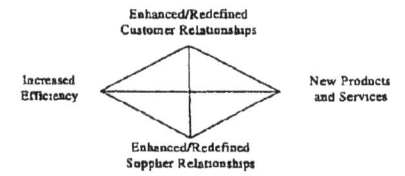

Most firms described e-business visions that had *evolved* as they learned about internet technologies, their customers or suppliers, and their own organizations. Each firm's initial vision usually focused on just one of the above four objectives, but visions evolved as e-business experience accumulated. Many firms started with efficiency-based initiatives, because they could be justified in quantitative terms (i.e. clear cost savings). For example, one firm developed a series of quick payback, efficiency-oriented initiatives by recording observed customer needs.

> *Each time a customer representative provides a service, they tick off what service was rendered. Those ticks are added up and ranked, and we're just starting at the top of the list, working our way down, offering features and functionality that will eliminate the most common requests.*
>
> —*Business Unit Vice President*

Success in one category of initiative invariably led to related initiatives in a different category. For example, at one firm an *efficiency*-focused effort that started with off-loading post-sale inquiries about orders from customer service employees on to customers eventually *redefined the relationship* between the customer and the customer service representative. The customer service unit at that firm now offers *completely new services* to customers. For example, they help customers redesign their purchasing processes so as to reduce or eliminate customers' need to inquire about orders.

> *We've transformed that group from being reactive to a very proactive organization driving satisfaction.*
>
> —*Director of Internet Commerce*

In summary, early e-business initiatives at the firms in our sample proved to be important learning experiences. They learned about their customers' habits, and they learned what those customers were—and were not—ready to do on the Web. They also tested new products and services and learned whether or not there was a market for them. And they learned about their organizational capabilities and limitations for doing business on the Web.

Strategic Levers

For most firms in our study, ingrained organizational processes were often at odds with e-business. Not surprisingly, most firms have not yet experienced radical changes in their organizational structures or business models. They have not suddenly morphed into e-business organizations. But, they have invested heavily in their IT infrastructures, revamped their governance structures, scrambled for IT competencies, overhauled their development methodologies, and relentlessly redesigned their business processes.

In a way, their efforts paralleled those of a couch potato attempting to become a body builder. That kind of transformation requires a whole series of changes in diet, lifestyle, and motivation. The future body builder can leverage existing strengths (e.g. muscle tone, coordination, stamina)—if any, but will need to secure facilities, devise a work-out plan, and develop the discipline to deliver on the plan.

Similarly, as these firms move from bricks-and-mortar to clicks-and-mortar, it appears that several elements must be aligned. We call these elements strategic levers, because each of them forces firms to deal with tensions that arise from simultaneously attempting to retain the strengths of an existing business model while dismantling characteristics that inhibit the transition to an e-business model. We observed three strategic levers (Figure 2):

1. An IT infrastructure that is simultaneously reliable, cost effective, and flexible,
2. Shared business/IT governance of e-business initiatives that encourages both consensus building and responsiveness to market demands and funds both applications and infrastructure,
3. Development that is both fast and reliable and that strategically applies internal and external sources of competence

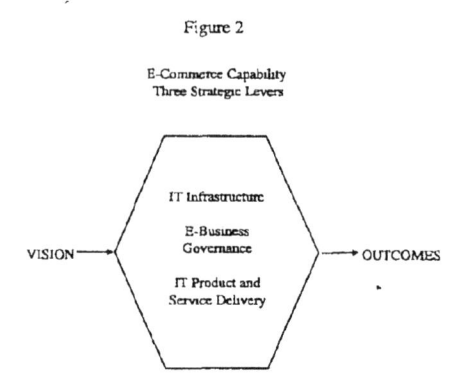

Figure 2

E-Commerce Capability
Three Strategic Levers

VISION → [IT Infrastructure / E-Business Governance / IT Product and Service Delivery] → OUTCOMES

We found an interdependence among these strategic levers, firms attending to all three of them were having more success in building their e-business competence. Just as the future body builder must resist the temptation to revert to old habits, firms were attempting to avoid old habits that would limit their effectiveness in an e-business environment.

In the remainder of this report, we describe the nature and implications of the three strategic levers at our sample firms.

The IT Infrastructure

What makes the IT infrastructure a strategic lever in the transformation to an e-business organization is that e-business has heightened the importance of a strong, shared technology base that allows the firm to project a single face to its global customers and integrates related processes across the organization. It highlights the need for a standardized, maintainable technology environment as well as the need to occasionally take advantage of the capabilities of important new or non-standard technologies. It also forces firms to invest simultaneously in solutions that will demonstrate a fast and highly visible payback as well as solutions that have a longer, less visible payback. And firms that have traditionally deployed

annual budgeting processes are finding that some e-business investments demand much more than a one-year commitment and others become irrelevant in much less than a year. To some extent, these challenges are not new. Indeed, some firms have been working on them for years, but few firms have learned how to address the inherent tradeoffs and balance the demands as they build their IT infrastructures. Compounding the challenge is the accelerating pace of change in business demands and information technologies. Firms must decide when to accept the risks associated with adopting new technologies and business opportunities and when to accept the risks of waiting until the technologies have matured and the business scenario is clearer.

Respondents agreed that their existing IT infrastructures had provided a starting point for e-business. However, all of them needed to expand their capabilities. Many made major investments to "seed" their e-business initiatives. These included some big investments in hardware, such as standardized desktops, revamped networks, and powerful servers, systems management tools that enabled them to move into true 24x7 operations, and foundation systems such as enterprise resource planning systems, electronic marketplace applications and data warehouses. Other firms had grown their infrastructures with smaller, incremental investments. As sample firms attempted—either expressly or tacitly—to address the tradeoffs in their infrastructure investment decisions, we identified four approaches to infrastructure investment that differed in their focus and objectives (See Figure 3.) These four approaches reflected different priorities as firms attempted to balance the requirements that e-business placed on their IT infrastructures.

Figure 3
Balancing Infrastructure Approaches

Focus

Future Unspecified	Standards *Cost*	Options *Learning*
Current Targeted	Deals *Benefits*	Capacity *Demand*
	Efficiency	Flexibility

Objective

Meeting Demand with Capacity. One approach was to invest in capacity. This involved providing baseline technologies, such as network bandwidth, firewalls, application development tools, and server farms. It also involved ensuring 24x7 system monitoring and management. Both IT and business respondents noted that e-business gives new meaning to the term 24x7. Most of the firms had, for some time, provided 24x7 *access* to their systems, but some had not provided 24x7 *management* of their systems (e.g. help desk). Others noted that they did not have enough capacity or redundancy to ensure that their systems could not fail or, if they did, that they could be rapidly recovered.

> *What still needs to be developed is the basic blocking and tackling for a robust system as we move from "you can get anything to work for 20 people." When you have thousands of people hitting the enter key at the same time, it's not going to work. That's a challenge. It's building scalability and redundancy. It's ramping up for 24x7.*
>
> —*IT Director*

In early e-business initiatives, requirements for network and hardware capacity tended to be hard to estimate because Web traffic was unpredictable. Several firms mentioned that their websites had failed because they had underestimated demand. Rather than over-invest in infrastructure technologies, the majority of companies attempted to closely monitor demand and build capacity that was just a little ahead of current needs. In other words, the capacity approach offered firms some flexibility to grow existing applications and, in some cases, provided a base for future applications, but it was mainly intended to support stated, near-term initiatives. Consequently, we observed that firms taking the capacity approach were *focusing on demand*, hoping to both ensure a payback on their investments and minimize the negative impacts of fast changing technologies.

Learning by Buying Options. An **options** approach to e-business infrastructure investment involved developing tool sets that might—or might not—be useful in future development efforts. Options enabled firms to "hedge their bets" given the uncertainty of technology and business change. Firms taking an options approach learned about Web technologies or built capabilities even though they were not sure when or if they would cash in on their investments. Firms invested in options under the assumption that the payoffs from those that are leveraged will easily outweigh those investments that do not bear fruit. At one firm, an options approach involved writing and testing APIs for core legacy application data during application maintenance. As the IT executive explained it, "While we have the patient on the operating table, we do some additional work." If the APIs are needed for future applications, the development work will be fast and cheap. If not, the firm has incurred a sunk cost.

Some firms had taken a "build it and they will come" approach to their core infrastructures so that they would not be vulnerable to sudden surges in demand. Others were building options in their IT skills, so that they could quickly convert new requirements by virtue of having the skills on hand. At those firms options were a mechanism for testing and learning new technologies. They provided flexibility to respond to unspecified future opportunities. Firms did not know which of their options would pay off, but they invested in options to shorten cycle time in those cases where new technologies, or linkages, or skills would be needed. Thus, investing in options involved *focusing on learning*.

Economizing via Standards. A number of respondents noted that the firm's approach to infrastructure was to invest in **standards**—technologies that would create a standardized, manageable environment for e-business. This meant identifying a limited set of technologies and tools that would form the foundation for e-business initiatives. Respondents cited three benefits of investing in a standards-based IT infrastructure. First, it reduced cost by reducing the number of people and variety of expertise required to manage operations. Second, it increased manageability by improving monitoring and trouble shooting,

and enabling staff to develop expertise in specific technologies Third, in some cases, it improved cycle time by limiting technology choice and simplifying integration across applications Technology and IT process standards were expected to facilitate cost-effective IT operations as well as integration of data across applications

> *We've had successes where we've been able to reduce people's costs by bringing in standardization That has given us credibility. The drool hits the table when they see the impact of standardization on their bottom line*
>
> —*CIO*

As firms invested in standard applications and technologies in conformance with a defined architecture, they were typically building an infrastructure to support changing and not altogether predictable systems requirements While some firms focused on hardware and operating system standards, a number of respondents identified their enterprise resource planning systems as a critical piece of their technology architecture because it was intended to standardize applications supporting core transaction processes and the interfaces to the data they generated At other firms the architecture specified middleware that would standardize the process for accessing data for new web applications Ensuring the reliability and cost-effectiveness of their infrastructures enabled some firms to funnel IT cost savings into strategic applications of IT Thus, investing in standards was intended to generate long-term efficiency benefits. It involved *focusing on costs*

Making Deals for Benefits. Deals constituted the fourth approach to e-business infrastructure investment Deals referred to building infrastructure on an as-needed basis to support individual business units' e-business projects. For example, at one firm the marketing director requested $1 million for the user interface for the firm's first major e-business venture The IT unit, which needed to build supporting infrastructure, eventually had to tack on another $5 million to the total project funding Although senior management was persuaded that the additional investment would ultimately support other e-business initiatives as well, the full $6 million investment was allocated for the single marketing department project, and was approved only because "the marketing VP stuck with us."

Respondents noted that, by attaching infrastructure to particular business initiatives, a deals approach increased the likelihood that a firm would see a quick payback on its infrastructure investments These respondents were sometimes uncomfortable investing in an enabling infrastructure. As one CIO noted

> *Building an enabling infrastructure is expensive and very long-term. We want fast payback. Things change too fast to invest very heavily in the future*

In a deals approach, infrastructure investments depended on pairing the cost with specific anticipated benefits, which meant that most deals had a near-term focus We think of deals as *focusing on benefits*

Combining the Approaches. As firms implemented infrastructure intended to support e-business, they had conflicting concerns, such as reliability and performance, speed of development, ability to integrate

applications, return on investment, and operating costs. No approach optimized all of these concerns. For example, the deals approach proved useful in getting the commitment of individual business units to take responsibility for generating benefits. However, a heavy reliance on deals often led to very sparse spending on a standard infrastructure. This limited firms' ability to develop cost-effective operations or to share learning across the organization. One e-business technology director lamented that as his firm's e-business initiatives expanded, it was becoming increasingly difficult to find ways to integrate them.

A heavy reliance on standards-based infrastructure investments improved the ability to integrate applications and contained operations costs, but it created a different problem. Specifically, firms that permitted standards to dictate investments risked limiting business flexibility. One e-business director complained that his IT unit, which was standards-driven in its design, was not responsive to customer demands. Others believed it was too early to settle on standards in the e-business arena. Firms that bought heavily into options and capacity infrastructure investment philosophies believed they were poised for rapid development. However, they risked spending large sums of money that might generate little or no return.

Not surprisingly, most of the firms in the study had taken multiple approaches to building e-business infrastructure. In fact, the ability and willingness to take multiple approaches appeared to be important to addressing the conflicting demands that e-business placed on the infrastructure. Deals most often dominated firms' approaches to infrastructure investment, because management sees them as the most effective means for assigning accountability for generating value. However, deals reinforce existing structures and processes. As they introduce e-business initiatives, many firms feel the need to reorganize or work more cross-functionally. Deals may work against that kind of change. In addition, deals encourage incrementalism. In a learning environment, incrementalism is an effective way to extend an infrastructure. However, if the existing infrastructure is weak, incremental investments may be very slow to pave the way for future opportunities.

Consequently, many firms needed an infusion of capacity funding to establish a reliable network, several described the importance of an ERP, or middleware as an investment in a standardized application environment even though they usually funded infrastructure with deals, and several firms invested in options, even though they did not describe them as such. Firms' dominant approaches tended to reflect their strategic e-business goals, whereas "exceptions" reflected the reality of competing objectives. Generally, infrastructure investments reflected an organization's learning about the demands of e-business.

> *We've had to make a fundamental recognition that to operate a web business you have to integrate your telephone, email and web communications into a seamless shopping experience for the customer. Without those three things combined, that's really a problem. It's a learning experience.*
>
> —*E-Business Head*

E-Business Governance Structures

Infrastructure investments constitute just one of the many decisions that influence a firm's e-business capability. E-business also creates tensions around organizational decision-making. On the one hand, firms wish to move quickly in the e-business arena and thus want rapid decision-making processes. On the other hand, they need to build understanding and consensus around new organizational initiatives and commitments, which can be enormously time-consuming. To ensure the reliability and predictability of their organizational actions, they want disciplined, standardized processes across some parts of the organizations, but they want empowered decision-makers leveraging those processes. Firms that have been experimenting with "federal" organizational structures have already started to address these issues, but e-business has created some unique twists on the tradeoffs between centralization and decentralization, standardization and empowerment, time-to-market, and consensus-building. Firms are addressing these through a variety of e-business governance structures. These governance structures attack some concerns about organizational processes while exacerbating others. Thus, e-business governance emerges as a second strategic lever.

We use the term governance to encompass the structural and process mechanisms that firms used to make e-business-related decisions and manage e-business initiatives. We identified four distinct models that firms used to address the inherent conflicts in e-business governance: IT-centric, New Venture, Status Quo, and Matrixed. These models can be characterized along four dimensions: (a) the organizational structure for managing e-business, (b) the source of investment funds, (c) the method by which funding for e-business initiatives was justified, and (d) the assignment of accountability for generating anticipated cost savings or new revenues. A table of the four models and their distinctive characteristics is shown in Figure 4.

Figure 4
Governance Approaches

	IT Centric	New Venture	Status Quo	Matrixed
Structure	E-business within IT	Large e-biz unit include IT	Minimal disruption	Changing roles & structures
Funding	CIO budget	Corporate funds unit	Business units	Steering committee
Justification	Standards & capacity demands	Strategic opportunity	Strategic necessity & ROI	Strategic opportunity & payback
Accountability	CIO	E-business head	Business units	Senior mgmt & business units

IT-centric Governance Model. The first governance model could be called an **IT-centric** approach. In this approach the firm's e-business unit was part of the IT organization and formally reported to the CIO. In most cases, the e-business unit was staffed with both IT and business professionals who designed and delivered e-business initiatives. Although there were variations in how these e-business units were funded, most often infrastructure investments were allocated by senior management from corporate funds

as part of the CIO's budget In some cases funds would be recovered through chargebacks to business units Over half of the IT-centric firms required financial justifications to support e-business infrastructure investments, but whether or not a financial justification was completed, most respondents noted that management viewed e-business investments as a strategic opportunity to build or leverage a technology competence

> *We consider this roadmap funding, justified on the basis that it gets us to where we want to go We still do an ROI but roadmap thinking is in the background. If it doesn't have an ROI, it better have a roadmap.*
>
> —*Director of E-commerce*

The accountability for the success of e-business initiatives at IT-centric firms rested with the CIO At most firms, members of the e-business unit reporting to the CIO also felt responsible for generating cost savings and incremental revenues Rarely did individuals outside the IT and e-business units have ownership of the e-business efforts in the firm.

Ten of our sample firms had an IT-centric governance approach and two others had recently changed from this arrangement. Several others indicated that they would eventually abandon the IT-centric model They credited this governance approach with creating a general awareness of the strategic importance of IT to the firm and with facilitating efforts to build an e-business infrastructure that provided visibility into the possibilities for e-business within their organizations Although all approaches to infrastructure investment were in evidence at IT-centric firms, this governance model was the most likely to emphasize a standardized infrastructure environment.

Most respondents in IT-centric firms felt that their early initiatives had generated intended cost savings and in some cases had improved customer relationships. However, respondents from these firms noted that they sometimes struggled to get the cross-functional cooperation they needed because the e-business unit had been somewhat isolated from the mainstream. In addition, several respondents complained that customers were slow to adopt new habits in response to their e-business initiatives. This may reflect the firm's own focus on technology in delivering new applications Thus, it appears that the IT-centric approach may yield important learning about how to deliver a Web-enabled product or service, but there is a risk that over time, e-business initiatives can get mired within IT and lack the kind of executive sponsorship required for firm-wide commitment Unless IT leadership can engage key business unit leaders, this governance approach may not represent a long-term solution.

New Venture Governance Model. A second governance model we identified was the New Venture This approach created a separate e-business unit combining IT and business unit expertise and reporting to a senior executive This unit had its own budget allocated by senior management, and senior management was most often heavily involved in overseeing its key initiatives The formation and continued funding of the venture, which was sometimes referred to as a "skunkworks," were usually justified as fulfilling a strategic opportunity Most of the respondents in the five firms that had adopted

this structure noted that the e-business organization provided opportunities to understand the viability of a dot-com idea

> *We can build a new service and wait for customers to tell us where we were stupid and how we can make it better. So we make sure the infrastructure is in place and then we build on it All the suggestions we get from customers help us deliver next versions that meet their needs*
>
> —*Vice President of Internet Services*

Accountability in the New Venture firms depended upon senior management's intentions for the e-business unit. In two firms, the unit was intended to remain separate from the firm's core business processes and thus responsibility for the success of these initiatives rested with e-business unit leadership In the other three firms, ownership of e-business initiatives was being shared with related business units As this sharing of responsibility with the rest of the organization was taking place, it was leading to major organizational change. For example, at one firm, a corporate marketing department had emerged, with a charter to focus on newly available Web products and services In the past, all marketing responsibility had been located within each strategic business unit; at this firm New Venture governance was leading to the adoption of entirely new organizational forms and functional relationships The New Venture model did not align with any particular infrastructure investment approach. We did not identify any particular trends in firms' use of the New Venture governance model One firm in the study had just announced that it would be moving toward this kind of structure We are not aware of any firms that had abandoned it or intended to do so

Status Quo Governance Model. A third governance model is best described as **Status Quo** This form of governance was intended to minimize disruption to an existing (usually quite successful) business organization At most of the seven firms that we characterized as taking a Status Quo approach, there was no formal e-business unit, although three of the firms had designated an e-business head who attempted to coordinate initiatives across business units In general, the Status Quo approach involved traditional project approval processes in which senior management—often through a steering committee—approved IT investments supporting e-business initiatives This approval was always based on financial return (e g , ROI or ROA), but respondents noted that the numbers were sometimes sketchy and senior management approval was probably motivated more by perceived competitive necessity than the merits of the numbers:

> *This might be a nuclear arms race thing that we have to do to be in the game All the major competitors have this When I talk to people who are doing [what we are] they tell me that they're not seeing any cost savings at all There's no reduction in service effort, just a change in what the customers ask for It may just be another thing we had to do not to be left out*
>
> —*Business Unit Vice President*

Although senior management approval was necessary, e-business investments in Status Quo firms were typically funded by the business units Accordingly, business units were generally responsible for generating benefits from their e-business investments In most of the Status Quo firms, senior management had not embraced e-business as an organizational priority In these firms, more so than any others in the study, respondents noted that resistance to change was an impediment to e-business success As a rule, these firms had adopted a pure *deals* approach to funding infrastructure, so they were struggling to get infrastructure funded While many of these firms' e-business initiatives had generated measurable benefits, several respondents observed that they needed some central leadership of the individual e-business efforts in order to achieve significant benefits

> *E-business [in our firm] is becoming increasingly centralized. It didn't start out that way I think e-business will become small and highly matrixed. For us the biggest change is trying to understand how you manage in a matrixed environment*
> —Vice President of Reengineering

Matrixed Governance Model. We refer to the fourth e-business model as **Matrixed** In contrast to IT-centric and New Venture approaches, in which business and IT competencies were housed in a single unit, with the Matrixed approach, e-business competencies are jointly assigned to one or more e-business units and the centralized IT services unit In some Matrixed firms, e-business is distributed across business units, like in the Status Quo model But the Matrixed firms are formally coordinating e-business competencies across business units Some of the firms using the Matrixed governance approach had e-business heads in each of their business units who then worked as an e-business team or committee to foster organization-wide efforts. At two smaller firms, the CEO was heading up e-business with significant input from the CIO Consequently, the Matrixed approach facilitated integration, joint accountability, and development of a shared infrastructure.

In Matrixed firms, some initiatives were justified on the basis of financial return, while others were viewed as a strategic opportunity Senior management had usually funded some shared infrastructure, taking either a *capacity* or a *standards* approach, but these firms also relied on *deals* to fund applications or other business initiatives in order to ensure that business unit managers had some "skin in the game"

> *People aren't [necessarily] strategically invested in what they ask for They have lots of ideas that are good for the business, but they have trouble delivering the value [Requiring them to pay for their applications] will help them stay focused. Corporate needs to know how the groups will deliver the value*
> – Business Unit Vice President

Business unit or senior managers accepted accountability for e-business success in Matrixed firms Perhaps because e-business efforts had a very high profile in these firms, respondents talked of large-scale organizational change, but not of resistance IT had become pervasive in Matrixed firms This led to greater access to information, which in turn, provided better understanding of both existing and new customers Respondents also noted that they were learning to become more customer-focused and

process-oriented This created a new emphasis on process integration, which was critical to their transformation into e-business organizations.

> *If you give a guy a set of carpenter's tools he doesn't immediately become a carpenter But a year after you give him the tools, he can do things he never imagined with those tools And I think it's that kind of explosion of learning that's starting to happen here as a result of process integration. We're starting to discover how in this integrated environment we're going to manage*
>
> —Vice President of Process Reengineering

Like the IT infrastructure alternatives, the four governance models that we've described here represent different preferences for balancing the tradeoffs. The IT-centric model allowed firms to thrust IT into a more strategic role and to focus on potential technology-related stumbling blocks The disadvantage of this model was the limited commitment that was evidenced outside IT The New Venture model is useful for encouraging more radical thinking about opportunities and freeing e-business teams from legacy processes The isolation of the New Venture model is a double-edged sword, however Innovations are more likely to prosper in the New Venture environment, but less likely to spill over into the rest of the organization Learning is fostered but isolated. The Status Quo approach permits slower change and may be most appropriate for firms that do not feel they can absorb major organizational changes, provided their industry is not rushing into e-business The Status Quo model is likely to be the least disruptive governance model, although respondents made it clear that individuals will feel and resist forced changes resulting from e-business Firms taking the Matrixed approach seemed farthest along in making organizational changes Their governance structures incorporate much of the "federal" organizational model

IT Product and Service Delivery

The third strategic lever is IT product and service delivery This is a critical lever because speed of delivery has become paramount

> *As cautious as I am professionally, this is an area in which I think you have to move very, very quickly If it's done properly, you can make a lot of money The paradigm today is speed not risk. [Speed] is the stumbling block.*
>
> —CIO

While some respondents argued that the need for speed was exaggerated, it was clearly true that the faster a firm delivered new applications, the faster it learned about e-business opportunities and its own capabilities But this need for speed had not diminished the importance of factors such as reliability and performance. On the contrary, as e-business "opened the window to our bad processes," respondents felt they had little margin for error as they expanded their e-business offerings

The emphasis on speed, accompanied by the visibility of poor performance, was leading to new practices for delivering IT products and services. Respondents noted that some of these practices made them uncomfortable

> *We are in the Stone Age with regard to IT We're starting to invest heavily in talent and even taking risks with regard to the kind of people we bring [in] These strategies are uncomfortable, very different from what we have traditionally done and what our culture is accustomed to Some of this makes my skin crawl, but we can't move the whole company as fast as we need to. We are partnering with people we never would have partnered with before The discomfort is from relying on some of these outsiders and the implications of trying to keep up with this fast-moving stuff*
>
> —*Vice President of Process Reengineering*

New approaches to delivering IT products and services were especially apparent in how firms were choosing to provide resources for e-business development and in their development methodologies

Competence Sourcing. As firms addressed tensions around cost, speed to market, strategic alignment, and the building of technical competencies, they were making decisions about the sourcing of the development of their e-business initiatives. At the time of the interviews some firms were outsourcing development because it was faster; others were doing development in-house for the same reason Some were outsourcing for cost reasons, others were developing in-house for the same reason They agreed that they did not want to outsource anything they did not understand, but it was difficult to develop systems in-house if they did not understand the technologies·

> *Generally the philosophy around here is that we would prefer to do things ourselves, especially if it's core or strategic or mission critical or proprietary or it takes knowledge or experience to do On the periphery, it can be outsourced. But given the pace we have had to move at, we need to push those conventions, to open up the categories of what can be outsourced. There is too much of this stuff that is new and fun and they'd rather learn about it The problem is that we don't have time for everyone to learn everything in advance We have to deliver first and then learn along the way*
>
> —*Head of E-business IT*

Many of the firms had outsourced early e-business application or web-site development because they did not possess the skills internally and they wanted to get something to market quickly Later, most of these firms brought some elements of e-business development back in-house both because they were concerned about the manageability of systems developed externally and because they felt that many of the skills required to deliver e-business applications represented critical competencies Most respondents stated that long-term they intended to use a combination of building, contracting, and outsourcing approaches. In the meantime, they were attempting to learn which competencies were, and which competencies were not, strategic The fact that key skills were in short supply had an impact on their sourcing strategies

There are some realities of the HR market that prevent us from building certain capabilities. In some cases, it just isn't economically feasible. We draw the line at where the customer touches the application. We're loathe to give up customer contact.
—*Director of Internet Technology Support*

Firms' decisions on sourcing e-business system development were not necessarily congruent with their sourcing decisions for ongoing operations. Several firms that intended to outsource all development were retaining operations, while others that had done most development internally were outsourcing operations like server and network management. Firms that retained operations usually felt that it was cost effective to do so, while those that chose to outsource pointed to the availability of bandwidth on demand and the increased reliability of networks and servers that were in the hands of outsourcers.

Development Methodology. A number of respondents indicated that the combined effect of fast-changing technologies and the demand for speed to market was creating a fundamentally different application development environment:

Our development people have developed an appetite for doing things quickly. We now have what I call the "hair on fire" group. They're dedicated to fast turnaround. They're getting their sense of self-worth from speed, not quality, which was the old culture.
—*Vice President of Information Technology*

In order to accommodate the new emphasis on speed, firms were purchasing packages, building applications in small increments, and shortcutting the quality and testing process. Respondents noted that "throw-away applications" allowed them to test new ideas and learn about customer preferences before they invested resources in building more robust applications. Some firms had public testing grounds for new applications that did not carry their firms' names.

Despite the emphasis on speed, IT units and their business partners felt it was important to manage risk. Some distinguished their firms from dot-com firms in that respect. At least one firm tested new processes manually prior to developing code that would automate the back-end to a Web interface. Another noted that each application required careful consideration of the risks of moving quickly.

It's a matter of executive leadership and negotiation—the problem has been finding the right balance between changing rapidly for the fastest time to market vs. the need for impeccable availability and performance at the 100% level. The faster you move, the less likely you are to have impeccable performance. The more you wait for perfect performance, the slower you are to market. The key is getting everyone to agree on the tradeoff you want to make and getting the leadership to make that decision and stick to it.
—*General Manager, Strategic Business Unit*

IT respondents said that Web applications naturally brought much greater involvement of business partners in IT management decisions. They observed that business managers were gaining an appreciation

of what was involved in making systems work. However, the possibilities offered by new technologies created constant pressures to change technology standards or to adopt immature technologies. In general, IT units discouraged the use of immature technologies. Still, they wanted to adopt new technologies quickly once they were believed to be robust, so some infrastructure managers focused on "developing an infrastructure in which it was possible to pull out one tool and put in another without undermining the existing infrastructure." One infrastructure director noted that his firm was comfortable taking risks with new technologies as long as there was an "exit strategy."

The sense of urgency was conveyed by respondents at most of the firms we interviewed, and this leads us to conclude that ongoing changes in most firms' development strategies will continue. One respondent noted that, "the normal development cycle is gone and nothing consistent has replaced it."

E-Business Enablers and Inhibitors

Our research suggests that developing an e-business capability is more a matter of implementation than strategy. Firms are learning by doing rather than by planning or talking. While every respondent was able to describe some kind of e-business vision, the net effect of their firms' efforts represented the cumulative learning that the firm had acquired through cycles of taking action, assessing the outcomes, and recalibrating. As one respondent noted

> *Understanding what you need to do is not rocket science and you don't have to build everything in the first go-round. The key is just doing it*
>
> *—Director of Internet Commerce*

It appeared, however, that some firms were further along the learning curve than others. Firms that had a combination of strong in-house IT skills, a tradition of investment in shared IT infrastructure, an architecture-based IT infrastructure reflecting the firm's need for integration, and shared goals across business and IT units enjoyed a head start in the process of transforming a bricks-and-mortar firm into a clicks-and-mortar firm.

Some firms' strengths had become their weaknesses. For example, firms that had developed strong EDI systems typically found that their customers were reluctant to abandon them in favor of Web-based systems. Similarly, some firms found that their customers were very attached to their phone and fax systems. One respondent noted that his entire firm was anxious to adopt e-business applications quickly, but his customers seemed indifferent. The resistance to abandon old habits was as apparent in customers as in each firm's own efforts to transform itself.

Other obstacles were cultural, based on traditions of autonomy or strong functional organizations that needed to become cross-functional in order to address customer demands. Some respondents expressed concern about management distraction, which resulted from mergers, emerging (but not e-business related) competitive forces, and changes in management. And firms shared concerns about their ability to select and implement new technologies and address the skill shortage.

These enablers and obstacles make it clear that some firms enter the e-business arena with a clear advantage. But individual firms' ability to identify and respond to opportunities will ultimately determine who is successful in the e-business world

Conclusion

This report has identified three strategic levers that firms can pull in order to develop the IT competence required for successful e-business strategies

- IT Infrastructures
- E-Business Governance Structures
- IT Product and Service Delivery

Underpinning these levers is the need for organizational learning to develop the capability to transform to meet the key e-business opportunities and threats faced by individual firms. Each lever poses a set of challenges that provide opportunities for firms to distinguish themselves. The kinds of challenges that successful firms will master include the following

- How to strategically deploy a combination of in-house and external IT talent;
- When to push customers to use new technologies and when to just listen and respond,
- How to combine the four approaches to managing the e-business IT infrastructure;
- How to encourage both rapid decision-making and widespread buy-in to those decisions,
- How to fund and justify e-business investments in a manner consistent with the firm's vision,
- How to measure learning and transformation to better direct future efforts, and
- How to transition to and manage a systems development life cycle for Web applications

In the next phase of this research, we will take a closer look at questions like these

Appendix
List of Participating Firms

Air Canada	FleetBoston Financial
Amtrak	GE Capital
Arcadia Group	HADCO Corporation
BCEE	IBM Global Services
Brady Corporation	Johnson & Johnson
C H Briggs	Karstadt
British Airways	S S Lazio
Cisco Systems	State of Maryland, DLLR
CompUSA	Manheim Auctions
Confindustria	Ostergaard
Delta Airlines	Pitney Bowes
DHL	Safeway Stores Plc
E I du Pont de Nemours and Company	Sprint
E-Chemicals	Transitions Optical
Elf Atochem North America	Yellow Freight

Printed in the USA
CPSIA information can be obtained
at www.ICGtesting.com
LVHW021606101023
760709LV00008B/364